Lord, We Sing Your Praise!

Written By: Kayleen Bobbitt

Illustrated By: Marilee Arntz

Published by EA Books Publishing, a division of
Living Parables of Central Florida, Inc. a 501c3
EABooksPublishing.com

This book belongs to:

Written by Kayleen Bobbitt
Illustrated by Marilee Arntz

For crystal cold,
confetti days,
Bright with bold
beginnings,

Lord,
we sing your praise!

January

February

For candy-coated, Cupid days,
Laced with hugs and kisses.

Lord,
we sing your
praise!

For energetic, emerald days,
Leaping into spring,

Lord,
we sing your praise!

MARCH

For breezy, blossoming,
bunny days,
Plump with precious
promise,

Lord,
we sing your
praise!

For delicate, delightful
dreamlike days,
Dancing on through spring,

Lord, we sing your praise!

June

For heaven-kissed
honeysuckle days,
Ringing with romance.

Lord,
we sing
your
praise!

Happy Birthday
America

For fiery, festive,
freedom days,
Spangling summer skies,

Lord, we sing your
praise!

For shimmering, sand-swirled,
seaside days,
Tickled by the tide,

Lord, we sing your
praise!

SCHOOL DAYS

For bustling, boisterous,
backpack days,
Tumbling into Fall,

Lord,
we sing your praise!

ABC 123

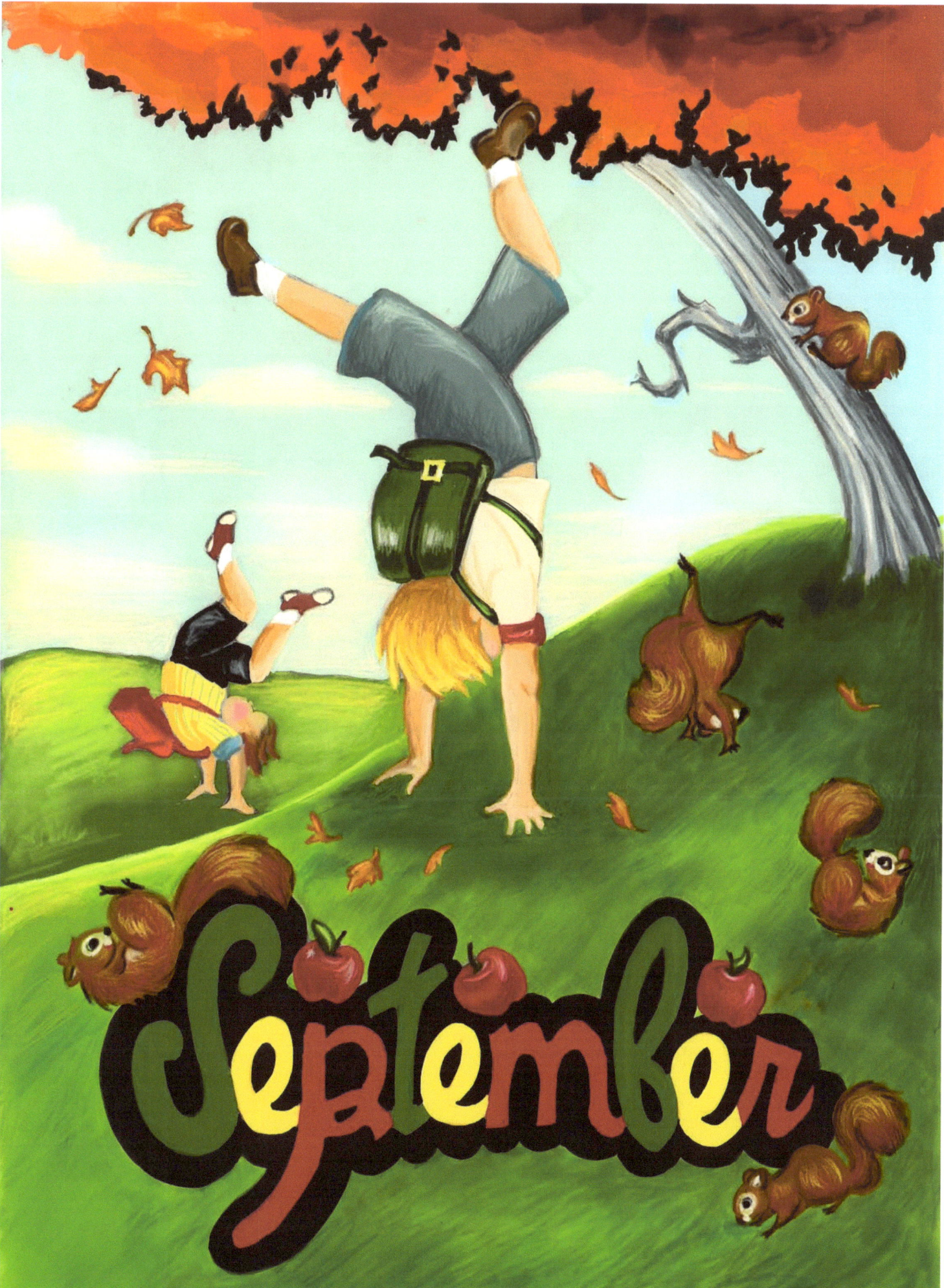

For sleepy, smokey,
autumn nights,
Bathed 'neath
the harvest moon,

Lord, we sing your
praise!

For taffy apple, turkey
days,
Trimmed with family,

Lord, we sing your
praise!

November

For wonderful winter
holidays,
Wrapped in heaven's
love,

Lord,
we sing
your praise!

DECEMBER

www.ingramcontent.com/pod-product-compliance
Lightning Source LLC
Chambersburg PA
CBHW060855270326
41934CB00002B/152